Butter Brains

Written by
Stephen Rickard

Illustrated by
Nicolas Rix

ransom

On a ship far, far off ...
Stand up! Now coil up this red cord and twist the end.
Then fix it to the box.
2

This is such
a good plan.
I think this will be
the best stunt
ever.

In a wet Welsh town, on the coast, Tim is on the job.
Quick, hop to it! We need to speed off with all this loot.
LOOT

Trust me. I can sort this.

Bad luck, Tim!
Bang!
6

Ow!
I cannot hear
a thing. My ears
are ringing.

Back on the ship ...
Point that thing at the target. Grab it tight and aim it.
Now press the power ... and off we go!
This melts brains as if they are butter. I cannot wait to see it start.

Beep! Beep!
ZZAP!
9

The "beep, beep" thing hits its target.
Look! This cannot be good!
My ears! The racket is too much!

Then ...

Such a lot of blank looks!

It looks as if that "beep, beep" thing might not be a load of rubbish.

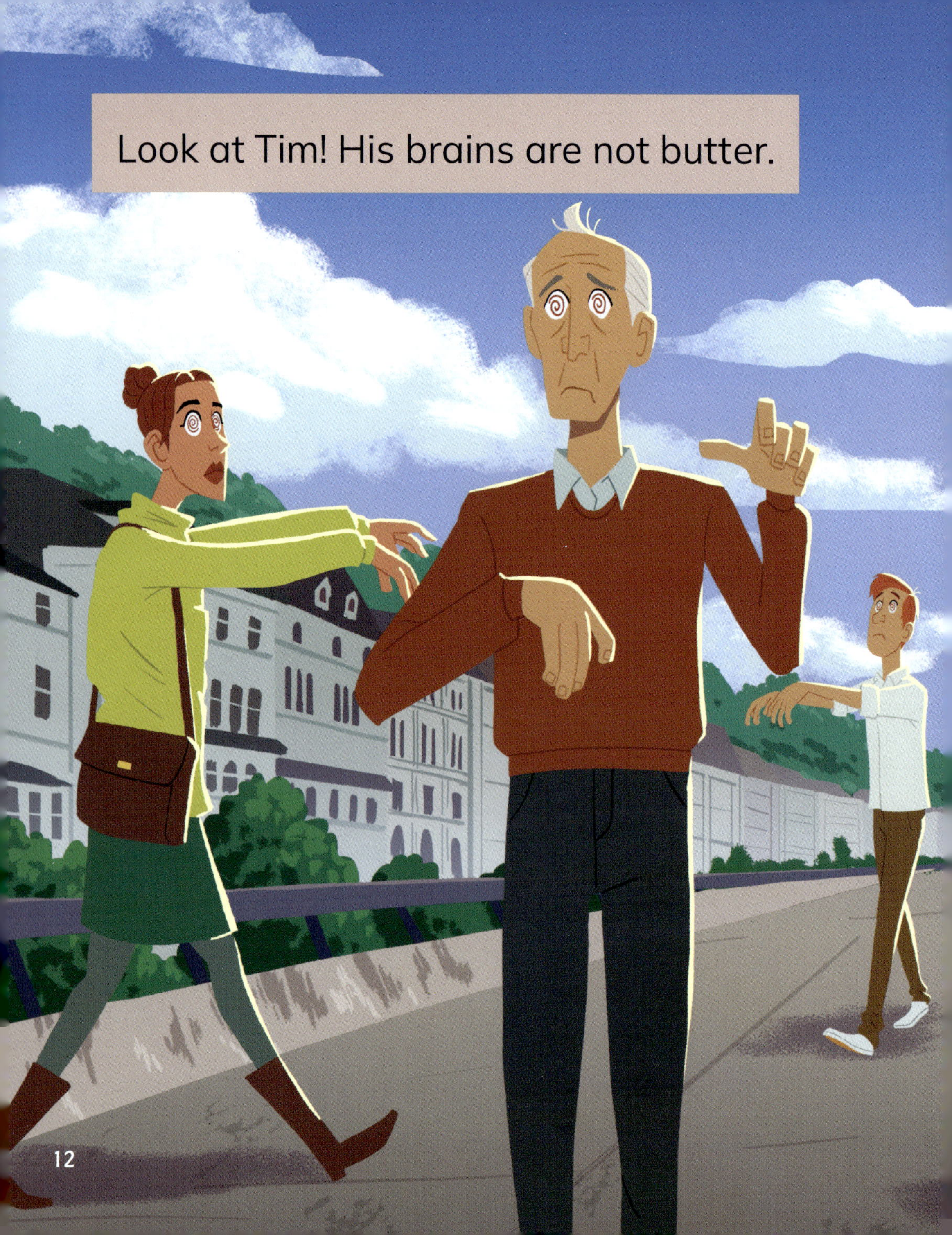

Look at Tim! His brains are not butter.

This is bad. I think I need to sort it.

Will Tim sort it? Can we trust him?

It looks like we can!
ZIP!

Good job, Tim. My brain is back.
You set us all free!
Are you chatting to me? I cannot hear a thing!